Favorites for Two

Arrangements by Pete Deneff

Disney characters and artwork © Disney
Disney/Pixar elements © Disney/Pixar

*Based on the "Winnie the Pooh" works, by A.A. Milne and E.H. Shepard

ISBN 978-1-70515-358-1

Visit Hal Leonard Online at
www.halleonard.com

Contact Us:
Hal Leonard
7777 West Bluemound Road
Milwaukee, WI 53213
Email: info@halleonard.com

In Europe contact:
Hal Leonard Europe Limited
42 Wigmore Street
Marylebone, London, W1U 2RN
Email: info@halleonardeurope.com

In Australia contact:
Hal Leonard Australia Pty. Ltd.
4 Lentara Court
Cheltenham, Victoria, 3192 Australia
Email: info@halleonard.com.au

THE BALLAD OF THE LONESOME COWBOY

from TOY STORY 4

TRUMPETS

Music and Lyrics by
RANDY NEWMAN

BE OUR GUEST
from BEAUTY AND THE BEAST

TRUMPETS

Music by ALAN MENKEN
Lyrics by HOWARD ASHMAN

BELLE
from BEAUTY AND THE BEAST

TRUMPETS

Music by ALAN MENKEN
Lyrics by HOWARD ASHMAN

Spiritedly

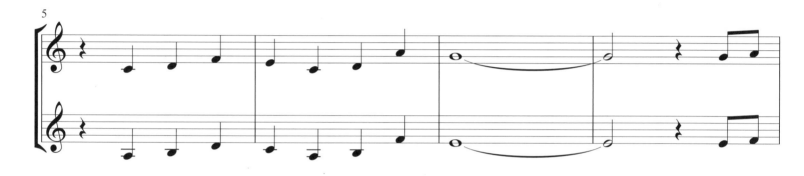

CRUELLA DE VIL
from 101 DALMATIONS

TRUMPETS

Words and Music by
MEL LEVEN

A DREAM IS A WISH YOUR HEART MAKES

from CINDERELLA

TRUMPETS

Music by MACK DAVID
and AL HOFFMAN
Lyrics by JERRY LIVINGSTON

Moderately

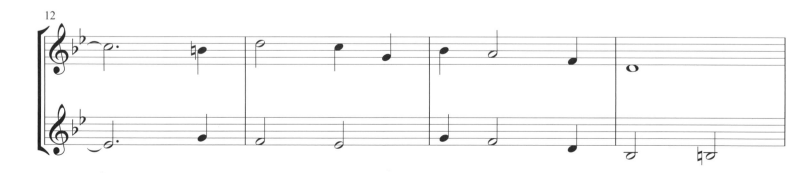

FOR THE FIRST TIME IN FOREVER

from FROZEN

TRUMPETS

Music and Lyrics by KRISTEN ANDERSON-LOPEZ
and ROBERT LOPEZ

HOW DOES A MOMENT LAST FOREVER

from BEAUTY AND THE BEAST

TRUMPETS

Music by ALAN MENKEN
Lyrics by TIM RICE

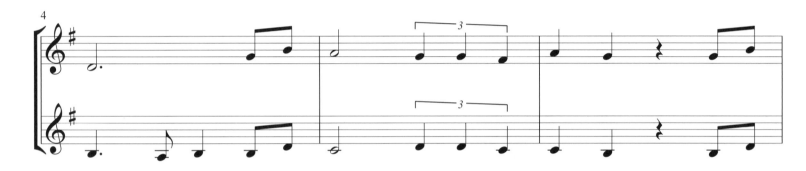

IN SUMMER

from FROZEN

TRUMPETS

Music and Lyrics by KRISTEN ANDERSON-LOPEZ
and ROBERT LOPEZ

INTO THE UNKNOWN

from FROZEN 2

TRUMPETS

Music and Lyrics by KRISTEN ANDERSON-LOPEZ
and ROBERT LOPEZ

JUST AROUND THE RIVERBEND

from POCAHONTAS

TRUMPETS

Music by ALAN MENKEN
Lyrics by STEPHEN SCHWARTZ

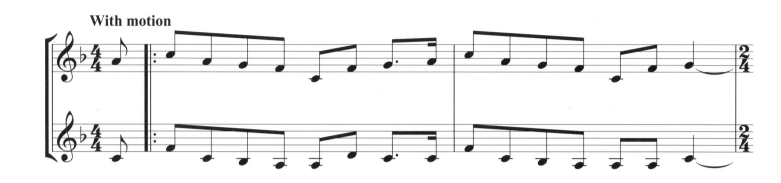

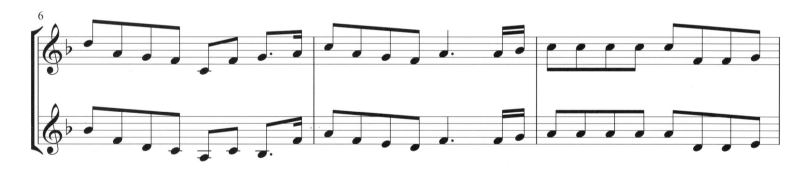

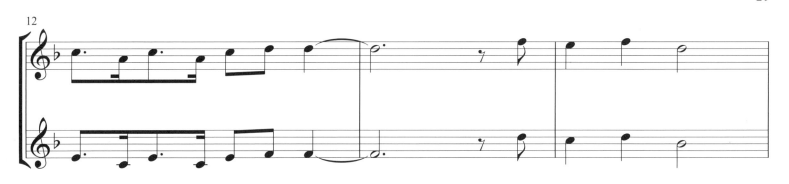

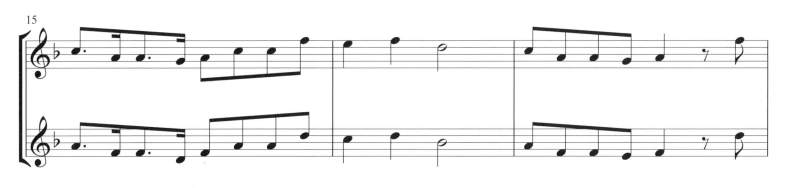

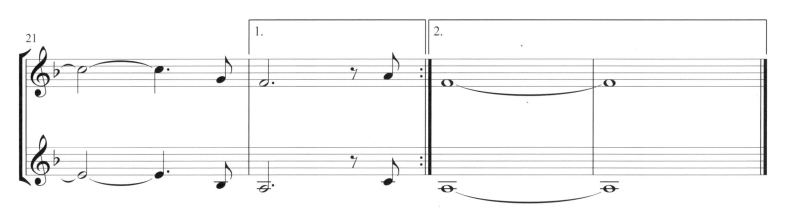

LAVA

from LAVA

TRUMPETS

Music and Lyrics by
JAMES FORD MURPHY

LEAD THE WAY
from RAYA AND THE LAST DRAGON

TRUMPETS

Music and Lyrics by
JHENÉ AIKO

NEVER TOO LATE

from THE LION KING 2019

TRUMPETS

Music by ELTON JOHN
Lyrics by TIM RICE

THE PLACE WHERE LOST THINGS GO

from MARY POPPINS RETURNS

TRUMPETS

Music by MARC SHAIMAN
Lyrics by SCOTT WITTMAN
and MARC SHAIMAN

REFLECTION
from MULAN

TRUMPETS

Music by MATTHEW WILDER
Lyrics by DAVID ZIPPEL

REMEMBER ME
(Ernesto de la Cruz)
from COCO

TRUMPETS

Music and Lyrics by KRISTEN ANDERSON-LOPEZ
and ROBERT LOPEZ

Moderately fast

SPEECHLESS
from ALADDIN

TRUMPETS

Music by ALAN MENKEN
Lyrics by BENJ PASEK
and JUSTIN PAUL

Moderately

THAT'S HOW YOU KNOW
from ENCHANTED

TRUMPETS

Music by ALAN MENKEN
Lyrics by STEPHEN SCHWARTZ

TOUCH THE SKY
from BRAVE

TRUMPETS

Music by ALEXANDER L. MANDEL
Lyrics by ALEXANDER L. MANDEL
and MARK ANDREWS

Quickly

TRY EVERYTHING
from ZOOTOPIA

TRUMPETS

Words and Music by SIA FURLER,
TOR ERIK HERMANSEN and MIKKEL ERIKSEN

UNDER THE SEA
from THE LITTLE MERMAID

TRUMPETS

Music by ALAN MENKEN
Lyrics by HOWARD ASHMAN

WINNIE THE POOH
from THE MANY ADVENTURES OF WINNIE THE POOH

TRUMPETS

Words and Music by RICHARD M. SHERMAN
and ROBERT B. SHERMAN

YOU'VE GOT A FRIEND IN ME

from TOY STORY

TRUMPETS

Music and Lyrics by
RANDY NEWMAN